My
MANIFESTATION
Journal

Set Your Intentions and
Manifest Your Desires

summersdale

MY MANIFESTATION JOURNAL

Text by Kitiara Pascoe

An Hachette UK Company
www.hachette.co.uk

Summersdale Publishers Ltd
Part of Octopus Publishing Group Limited
Carmelite House
50 Victoria Embankment
LONDON
EC4Y 0DZ
UK

www.summersdale.com

Printed and bound in the Czech Republic

ISBN: 978-1-80007-829-1

Substantial discounts on bulk quantities of Summersdale books are available to corporations, professional associations and other organizations. For details contact general enquiries: telephone: +44 (0) 1243 771107 or email: enquiries@summersdale.com.

Name:

....

Date of birth:

....

Journal start date:

....

Goals for your manifestation journey:

....

....

....

INTRODUCTION

Welcome to *My Manifestation Journal*, a place to focus your manifestation practice and learn new tips and exercises to aid your journey. In these pages, you'll learn about the history of manifestation, and what the law of attraction is, as well as lots of great techniques for realizing your biggest hopes and dreams. As you work your way through, you'll find quotes, affirmations and inspiring advice that will keep you on track and ensure you fulfil all your desires.

When you begin manifesting, you open yourself up to the infinite opportunities and power the universe has for you. You'll soon start noticing things you didn't before, turning negativity into positivity and discovering high-frequency people and activities. You can turn to this journal whenever you want, but regular practice will yield the best results.

Congratulations on starting your manifestation journey and taking the first steps towards building the life you've always wanted.

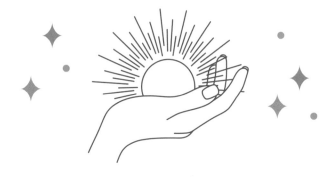

WHAT IS MANIFESTATION?

At its core, manifestation is the act of bringing into your life what you desire using thoughts and energy. By articulating in your mind exactly what it is that you want – be it a job, a relationship or even a material object – manifestation exercises help send your desires out into the universe, allowing those desires to manifest themselves in your life. Through manifestation, you open yourself up to the power of the universe and to the opportunities waiting for you.

There's no magic involved here, and manifestation isn't as simple as picturing a sports car and seeing it appear on your driveway. Instead, the practice shifts your energy levels to the things you desire, allowing you to better see the opportunities to acquire them and actively drawing them into your life.

An intentional practice, manifestation is based on something called the law of attraction.

The law of attraction

You might remember from school that the universe is packed with energy, and that energy can be altered but never destroyed. That's the First Law of Thermodynamics. The law of attraction is the concept that energies of the same frequency are drawn together or, in other terms, *attracted* to each other. It's easy to see this in action. People with high energy tend to be friends with other high-energy people. Energy can't be still, and as a result, all energy is constantly vibrating at a particular frequency. Even inanimate objects that seem to be still are in constant motion, their atoms and molecules vibrating together. When it comes to the law of attraction, it's thought that things that vibrate with similar frequencies are attracted to each other – this is where manifestation comes in.

Through thoughts and practice, manifestation allows you to change your frequency to that of the things you desire. As a result, that new job or friendship will find itself drawn to you. As a rule, positive things operate on higher frequencies while negative things have lower frequencies.

A BRIEF HISTORY OF MANIFESTATION

The idea that our thoughts create our realities is far from new and certainly isn't exclusive to manifestation and the law of attraction. Many cultures and religions, from antiquity to the present day, understand that how we think has a considerable effect on what happens to us and how we experience the world. This includes the ancient Romans and Greeks, as well as Hindu and Buddhist cultures. When it comes to specifically manifesting our desires, though, the concept arose with New Thought, a movement started in the US around the beginning of the nineteenth century.

The mesmerist and inventor Phineas Quimby is often said to be the founder of manifestation, although others had already theorized that some kind of conscious magnetism existed. Quimby, born in 1802, believed that he cured his own tuberculosis through the power of positive thinking and manifestation, and set about curing others of their perceived health issues.

Another member of the New Thought movement in the US, Prentice Mulford, was the first to explain the law of attraction in the late 1800s. Published around the turn of the twentieth century, Mulford's book, *Your Forces and How to Use Them*, changed the focus of manifestation. With the law of attraction, he argued, you can bring not only good health into your life but anything you desire, from wealth and possessions to relationships.

Self-help ideas start spreading

As these ideas began spreading among thinkers and philosophers, more works were published on the topics of manifestation and the law of attraction. William Walker Atkinson's book, *Thought Vibration or the Law of Attraction in the Thought World*, was one of the first to deal with the now-famous law.

Another author, Wallace Delois Wattles, was responsible for further popularizing the concept with the publication of his book, *The Science of Getting Rich*, in 1910. Expanding on Quimby's work and ideas, Wattles applied the concepts to wealth generation. Wattles also practised creative visualization, one of the key exercises in manifestation. He created strong images in his mind of what he wanted before intentionally working towards making that vision a reality. This, in essence, is exactly what manifestation is.

Self-help grows

One of the most famous books to espouse the law of attraction is Napoleon Hill's 1937 classic, *Think and Grow Rich*. One of the most successful personal wealth books in history, this timeless guide instructs the reader on creating a wealthy life through visualization, planning and perseverance. Countless financial gurus and CEOs point to this book as one of their inspirations in work and life.

Onwards into the 1980s, Louise Hay published *You Can Heal Your Life* and helped grow the self-help and New Thought literary genres. Like Quimby over a century earlier, Hay wrote that disease and ill health are rooted in negative mental thoughts, patterns and stress, emphasizing that anybody can take control of their health through positive thought techniques.

The Secret

Perhaps the most famous work of manifestation and the law of attraction is the 2006 documentary and book, *The Secret*, by Rhonda Byrne. It catapulted the concepts into public consciousness around the world, aided by the documentary's interviews with notable people who attributed their success to the law of attraction.

As the concepts of manifestation and positive thinking have become more widely known, numerous public figures and celebrities have spoken about their own techniques. From Jim Carrey revealing how he manifested his career from a young age, to Oprah Winfrey declaring that she's used the law of attraction in her career, these powerful techniques have left the niche New Thought movement and entered everyday parlance and use, allowing anybody to harness this universal power.

HOW TO MANIFEST

One of the best things about manifesting is that you don't need much to begin. In fact, a quiet space, a pen and this journal already put you in the perfect position to begin manifesting. As manifestation has become increasingly popular, you'll see tips across the internet and social media. Twitter, Instagram and TikTok all have popular posts inspiring you on your manifestation journey. It can be a little confusing at first, so let's break it down here.

There are five fundamental principles to manifesting:

1. Create a clear vision of what you desire.

2. Visualize your desire (or script it).

3. Identify your manifestation blocks – obstacles in your path.

4. Action your plan.

5. Believe the universe is listening.

The language of manifestation

Let's take a look at some of the lingo that you're likely to come across.

- Affirmation: A short phrase or mantra that you can repeat to yourself to change your mindset (e.g. "Money flows freely to me").

- Visualization: Creating vivid images in your mind of being in possession of what you desire as if it were real.

- Scripting: A technique involving writing down what you desire as if you already have it or in a way that says it's definitely coming to you (e.g. "A promotion is in my immediate future").

- **Frequency:** While manifesting, you can listen to ambient music on the frequency of the thing you desire to help raise you to that frequency.

- **Manifestation blocks:** Any obstacle that prevents you from achieving your manifestation. Negative beliefs, toxic people and opposing habits are common examples.

- **"Ask the universe":** This is a common phrase that refers to the act of sending your desire out into the universe, usually through a technique like affirmations, scripting or visualization.

Embracing the five principles

Manifestation is as straightforward as following the five principles in order, although that's not to say it's *easy*. Focusing, adjusting your mindset and visualization all require practice. Here's a summary of the five principles so you can start manifesting.

Principle One: Get clear on what you desire

You might think that you want the latest smartwatch, but when you dig deeper, it's really a desire to become fitter and healthier. Or perhaps you think a promotion will fix work frustrations, whereas articulating your desires reveals that you want to retrain in a different role entirely. Often, negative beliefs and fear cloud our vision, making us scared to admit what we really want. And don't forget, manifestation isn't just for jobs, health and material objects; you can manifest things like confidence, self-love and awareness too.

Principle Two: Visualize or script what you desire

When you imagine mental images using multiple senses, your brain begins living that vision as though it were real, helping to align your thinking. You'll find powerful visualization techniques throughout this journal.

Principle Three: Identify manifestation blocks

If you think it's impossible that you'll ever achieve your desires, affirmations can prove a powerful tool in fighting doubt. Choose one or two affirmations that shift you from doubt to belief (e.g. "The universe is ready to give me what I desire", or "I deserve everything I desire").

Other manifestation blocks include toxic influences and impatience. If you have relationships that deflate you and lower your energy levels, it might be time to distance yourself from those people. If you're flitting between manifestations because you feel impatient, remind yourself that the universe knows when the best time to grant your desire is, and trusting it is key.

Principle Four: Action your plan

The universe helps you achieve your desires, but it's a team effort and you need to put in the work. This means taking appropriate steps; for example, joining a club to help you meet new people.

Principle Five: Believe the universe is listening

The universe isn't a take-out service; there's no ten-minute delivery slot. Once you've got a clear vision of your desire and are taking steps towards it, it's time to trust that the universe has heard you and is working on providing you with what you've asked for.

HOW TO ADOPT A MINDSET
TO BEGIN MANIFESTING

While it would be nice to simply visualize what we want and have it appear, there's a little more to manifestation, starting with creating the right mindset. Most of us know that our mindset affects how we perceive things. If you're in a bad mood in the morning and your colleague asks you for a report, your negative mindset could make you see that request as an unreasonable demand. On a day where you're happy and uplifted, you could interpret the same request as a compliment. The same goes for approaching manifestation – by bringing the right mindset to it, you're far more likely to succeed in your goals.

So, what kind of mindset do you want to cultivate?

Become open and positive

Have you ever caught yourself saying "I could never do that", "I'm not clever enough for that" or another iteration of these negative beliefs? We're often our own worst critics. If you tell the universe you want your dream partner but simultaneously believe that you're not worthy of them, it's hard for the universe to give you what you want. By creating an affirmation routine that opens your mind to higher possibilities, your new, positive mindset will attract other positives into your life.

Start believing

There is a term in psychology called cognitive dissonance. It refers to the internal conflict that arises when a person's behaviour doesn't align with their beliefs. This conflict creates a block when it comes to manifestation. No matter how often you say affirmations or visualize your goal, you aren't succeeding because you don't believe in the process. This isn't the only reason you might not be seeing results, but it is a common one. Believing that manifestation works raises your frequency to match the positive things you desire.

Take control

There is one thing above all that will help you manifest successfully: taking control. The universe has your back and is supporting your desires, but it's only when you make the decision to take the first step that you will be able to switch your mindset from "I wish" to "I will".

MY
MANIFESTATION
JOURNAL

WHAT WOULD YOU DO
IF NOBODY WAS WATCHING?

We live in a world where media messages are constantly telling us how we should look, what we should own and how we should spend our time. As a result, it can be pretty difficult to differentiate what we actually want from what we *think* we should want. This can be a big obstacle when trying to articulate what we want from the universe. To combat this, here's a thought exercise for you.

Whatever realm you're focusing on – work, love, money, material objects – imagine how you would live that aspect of your life if nobody was watching. You can tailor the questions to yourself and your own desires, but here are a few examples (it's good to imagine that money is no object here too):

- What work would I want to do if nobody else knew?

- What clothes would I wear if nobody could see me?

- What make-up would I put on if nobody was looking?

These types of questions can be revealing: perhaps you'd wear bright-red lipstick or leopard-print jumpsuits. Perhaps you'd work for an animal charity or be a tour guide in the Sahara. It's easy to forget how influenced we are by what we think others are thinking about us.

What would you like the confidence to do, wear or say?

....

....

....

....

....

What do you truly want for yourself.

....

....

....

....

....

What type of person do you typically notice and admire?

....

....

....

....

....

How do you feel after you do something you're afraid of?

....
....
....
....
....

Which five things are you grateful for today?

....
....
....
....
....

What did you ask the universe for today?

....
....
....
....
....

You get in life what you have the courage to ask for.

OPRAH WINFREY

CREATE YOUR VISION BOARD

When you've got a clear understanding of what you're going to ask the universe for, creating a vision board is a popular way to visualize your desire and send it out into the world. Not only does the act of creating the vision board itself compound and focus your intentions, but it's also easy to refer back to on a daily basis to remind yourself exactly what your goal is.

You can make your vision board in two ways: either create it as a physical object using printed images, handwritten words and magazine cut-outs, or create it digitally using a platform such as Pinterest or another app where you can easily pool images together. A digital version on your phone has the added benefit of being accessible wherever you are, but don't dismiss a physical board – the hands-on act of creating it can be both therapeutic and intentional.

Whichever medium you choose for your board, here are some ideas for images, graphics and words to include:

- Images of people you associate with your goal.

- Colours that remind you of your goal.

- Words and phrases that inspire and push you towards what you want.

- Pictures of your desired object, be it a house, a job (perhaps use the company logo) or greater wealth.

- Uplifting, positive images, such as smiling and laughing people.

How does your dream life look?

....

....

....

....

....

....

....

....

....

....

In six months' time, what's the one thing you want to be or have?

....

....

....

....

....

What three things are you grateful for today?

....

....

....

What did you ask the universe for today?

....

....

....

....

How do you feel after today's practice?

....

....

....

....

....

MAKE IT UNAVOIDABLE

When it comes to manifesting successfully, it's not just a case of one-and-done. You must focus on what you want every single day, even if it's just for five minutes in the morning and five minutes in the evening. A great way to do this is to make it unavoidable so it quickly becomes part of your daily life. We are what we repeatedly do.

Sometimes the simplest way to make your desire unavoidable is to use the king of stationery: the mighty sticky note. Write your goal, or a word that reminds you of your goal, on a sticky note and place it somewhere you look several times a day. Near the kettle or kitchen sink, on your computer screen or on your bathroom mirror are all great places. If you want it to remain private, you could draw a little doodle that represents your goal or use a code word.

What will you focus on manifesting this week?

....

....

....

....

....

Where will you put your manifestation reminder?

....

....

....

....

....

What time every day will you read your manifestation reminder?

....

....

....

....

....

What five things are you grateful for today?

....

....

....

....

....

What would you like to say to the universe?

....

....

....

....

....

What's one thing you can do now to raise your frequency?

....

....

....

....

....

I CHOOSE
TO LET GO
OF ANY
RESISTANCE

ARE YOU HOLDING YOURSELF BACK?

When we see highly successful people, it appears as though they've always been confident, well dressed and sure of themselves. Let's remember though, we're only seeing them at their best. Not only are we not seeing them when they wake up at 5 a.m. because their child is sick, but we're not seeing them as they were *before* they attained the success we know them for. The gap between where we are and where they are feels impossibly enormous. But comparing the start of your journey to a high point of theirs won't help your mindset.

A great way to improve your mindset is to understand that everybody is on their own journey to success. You can do this by reading the origin stories of the people who inspire you. While media might be geared towards famous folk, don't underestimate the power of getting in touch with others who inspire you. If you'd love to get a book published, why not reach out to a local author? If there's a role you want to eventually become qualified for, why not contact someone already in that role? This helps you realize that they're not better than you, merely at a different stage of their journey. It'll also help you build a network of connections focused around what you want. This can help free you from self-doubt and feelings of inadequacy.

Which five people inspire you?

....

....

....

....

....

Who are three people you could reach out to for advice?

....

....

....

Who seems to be living your dream life and why?

....

....

....

....

....

What three things are you grateful for today?

....

....

....

....

....

What are three steps you took to reach something you've already achieved?

....

....

....

....

....

What are three pieces of advice you'd give to someone who wanted your role?

....

....

....

....

....

LOOK INTO YOUR PAST

For this manifestation exercise, you're going to be making a list of all the things you have manifested in the past. Of course, you may not have realized at the time that you were manifesting, but now that you know what the law of attraction is, perhaps in hindsight you can see more clearly.

You can use your computer, phone, a piece of paper or this journal to begin. If you need a nudge to get those memories flowing, here are some questions to consider:

• Has anyone ever given you something you really wanted while being unaware you wanted it?

• Have you ever been thinking about an old friend and they suddenly get in touch?

• Have you ever lost something – maybe a role or relationship – and soon after landed a dream job or partner?

Often, what we've manifested shows up in a slightly different form than we might have envisaged. This is because the universe knows when the time is right and what version of your desire is best. Perhaps you're turned down for a pay rise but get a new title instead, prompting a headhunter to get in touch and offer a bigger salary. Think about your high points from a few angles and you might be surprised by what you discover.

What's the biggest "coincidence" you've ever experienced?

....

....

....

....

....

Describe a time when something felt like fate.

....

....

....

....

....

Write down a time when something difficult led to something wonderful.

....

....

....

....

....

What five things are you grateful for today?

....

....

....

....

....

Who would you love to hear from in the next week?

....

....

....

....

....

What would you like to manifest today?

....

....

....

....

....

I GIVE MYSELF
PERMISSION
TO HAVE
ANYTHING
I WANT

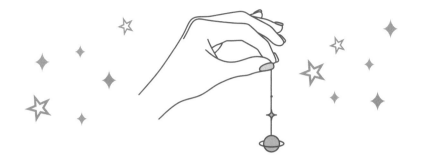

CREATIVE VISUALIZATION SESSION

One of the most popular manifestation techniques is creative visualization. The idea is to set your mind and your energy to the levels they need to be at to gain what it is you desire. Just like imagining your favourite food makes your mouth water, imagining the thing you desire helps to match its frequency and prepare you to receive it.

For creative visualization, it's best to find a quiet space where you won't be disturbed. Ideally, you want to practise this visualization several times a day, but just once is fine.

Follow these steps:

- Sit in a comfortable position that you can maintain for around 10–15 minutes.

- Close your eyes and take a few cycles of deep, slow breaths.

- Bring into your mind's eye a detailed image of what you desire.

- Imagine that you have that exact thing.

- Consider how you feel with it in your possession; what emotions are going through you?

- Create as much detail as possible, including sights, sounds, smells and sensations.

- When you're finished, hold on to those feelings for as long as possible.

- Repeat often, at least once a day.

What would you like to visualize?

....

....

....

....

....

What can you hear in your visualization?

....

....

....

....

What expression do you have on your face?

....

....

....

....

What are you wearing in your visualization?

....

....

....

....

....

How do you feel in your visualization?

....

....

....

....

....

How do you feel after today's practice?

....

....

....

....

....

MANIFESTATION ACCESSORIES

To get yourself into the ideal headspace for creative visualizing, you can take a few simple steps to make your environment as conducive as possible.

Music

As the law of attraction uses frequencies to draw your desires to you, switching your frequency is an important step. Listening to music at the right frequency can help you reach your goals. The best option isn't your favourite pop song, but a more blissful, ambient sound. Simply search the frequency on a music website like YouTube or Spotify.

174 Hz: calm	**285 Hz**: healing and rejuvenation
396 Hz: removing negativity	**417 Hz**: change and growth
528 Hz: love	**639 Hz**: communication
741 Hz: creativity	**852 Hz**: spirituality
963 Hz: simplicity	

Scents

There is no single scent that is best for manifestation, and different scents support different aims. Sage, mint, lavender and patchouli are popular, while bergamot and lemon are great for uplifting your energy in general. You can burn incense or use essential oils to fill the room with a gentle note.

Crystals

Many people enjoy using crystals as part of their manifestation practice as the crystal's energy supports their own. Clear quartz is a good general crystal for boosting vibrations. As crystal mining causes environmental damage, shop sustainably in second-hand shops. You can even use manifestation and visualization to find second-hand crystals.

What would you like to manifest today?

....

....

....

What frequency of sound would most closely match your goal?

....

....

....

How does it feel to be manifesting the life you want?

....

....

....

Who will you tell first about your successes in manifestation?

....

....

....

How will it feel to share your successes?

....

....

....

MY LIFE IS FILLED WITH LIGHT AND LOVE

CREATE A GRATITUDE JOURNAL

A gratitude journal is a powerful tool in manifesting as it helps raise your energy and brings positivity into your day. You can use a digital journal, although many people find the act of handwriting therapeutic, so using a paper notebook is a great idea as well. Of course, if you like writing but want to build a gratitude practice on the go too, you can do both!

A gratitude journal is a bit like a diary in the sense that it has dated entries. You can keep it as brief as you like and just write one thing you're grateful for each day, or write lists as often as you want. The main thing to remember is to spend a moment on each thing you're grateful for. Be present in the moment, and let the gratitude fill you up. You'll know when it's working because you'll likely feel a surge of happiness. There's no need to worry about forgetting something, as leaving something off the list doesn't mean you're not grateful for it.

Here are a few examples:

- I'm grateful for my best friend.

- I'm grateful the sun is shining today.

- I'm grateful for the birds in my garden.

- I'm grateful that my neighbours say hello every morning.

What ten small things are you grateful for?

··

··

··

··

··

··

··

··

··

··

What ten big things are you grateful for?

....

....

....

....

....

....

....

....

....

....

AFFIRMATIONS

One of the core techniques of manifestation and the law of attraction is affirmations. Even if you're new to manifesting, you've likely heard of affirmations before and even felt their power. They are short, uplifting phrases, and repeating them regularly can change your life. When choosing which affirmations to use, consider the thing you're currently manifesting and any blocks that you might have. For instance, if you want to manifest good relationships but feel deep down like you are unworthy, affirmations can help you succeed. Here's an example for this situation:

- "I am worthy of love."

- "I'm so grateful for the huge amount of love that surrounds me."

- "I love myself and am ready to give love to others."

Affirmations work best when you repeat them on a daily basis, usually more than once a day. While negative thoughts are normal, they can really hold you back. Saying affirmations every day helps replace negative thoughts with new, positive ones. As your energy rises with the positivity and is no longer held back by negative thoughts, not only will you be in a better place to spot romantic opportunities, but potential partners get to meet someone who believes in themself.

Four affirmations for love/relationships:

....

....

....

....

Four affirmations for self-belief:

....

....

....

....

Four affirmations for health/fitness:

....

....

....

....

Four affirmations for spirituality:

....

....

....

....

What three things are you grateful for today?

....

....

....

....

What would you like to say to the universe?

....

....

....

....

Every one of us needs to show how much we care for each other and, in the process, care for ourselves.

DIANA, PRINCESS OF WALES

MAKE AN INTENTION JOURNAL

Even after you've decided on what to manifest and begun using affirmations and visualization, you might feel a little lost when it comes to direction. Remember, the universe is set on helping you, but it can't do it alone. An intention journal is a space where you write down your intentions related to your manifestation goals, allowing you to clearly articulate to the universe what you want. Writing regularly is best – every day is ideal – and you don't need to write a lot, just a few clear intentions for your day, week or month.

If you're manifesting wealth, for example, your intentions will be geared towards the following:

- I intend to track all my spending this week.

- I intend on opening a new savings account this month to make room for my new wealth.

- I intend on asking my boss for a pay rise this week because I am worth more than I receive currently.

There is no pass or fail here though, you're simply setting out intentions so that the universe knows to support you with them. If they don't happen within the timeframe, perhaps the universe knew it wasn't quite the right time.

Five intentions you have for today or this week:

....

....

....

....

....

Five intentions you have for this month:

....

....

....

....

....

Five intentions you have for this year:

....

....

....

....

....

What three things are you grateful for today?

....

....

....

How do you feel after today's practice?

....

....

....

....

....

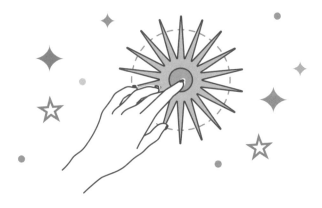

FIND HIGH-FREQUENCY FRIENDS

Do you know somebody who always leaves you feeling inspired, even if they haven't specifically been trying? Perhaps they listen closely to what you say and offer enthusiastic support, or maybe they recount stories of overcoming difficulty without taking themselves too seriously. Whatever it is about them, whenever you're in their presence you feel like anything is possible. This is a high-frequency person.

When you're in the presence of a high-frequency person, your frequency rises to meet theirs and you're suddenly more likely to spot opportunities, step outside of your comfort zone and take on challenges you might have thought were beyond you. Their high frequency quiets negative thoughts and helps bring your potential to the surface. Isn't it a fantastic feeling? Imagine if you were around high-frequency people *most of the time.*

The great thing about these people is that they're typically kind, generous and welcoming, so you don't need to be afraid of approaching them. To meet high-frequency friends and colleagues, head to environments they enjoy. These include networking events, group fitness classes, co-working spaces, book launches and other events. It's worth noting that high frequency isn't the same as extroverted; plenty of high-frequency people are introverts too.

Another option is to listen to podcasts by high-vibe people and read books by them. These give you instant access to their high-frequency personalities!

How does being around high-frequency people make you feel?

....

....

....

....

....

Four people you know who are high frequency:

....

....

....

....

How might you meet more high-frequency people?

....

....

....

....

....

How can you regularly surround yourself with more high-frequency people?

....

....

....

....

....

What five things are you grateful for today?

....

....

....

....

....

What would you like to manifest today?

....

....

....

....

....

I AM
CONFIDENT
AND
SUCCESSFUL

STEP AWAY FROM
LOW-FREQUENCY PEOPLE

Moving on from relationships that aren't working can be tough because there are often a lot of emotions involved, including guilt. However, when you have a friend, partner or acquaintance who has persistent low frequency, their energy can drag yours down. You know this happens when you speak to them and leave the conversation feeling deflated; when you've told them good news and they've undermined it; when you're hopeful and they tell you your plans won't work out; or if they spend all their time complaining or gossiping. While it's natural for us all to complain sometimes or to gossip about others, it becomes a problem when we indulge in these behaviours too often.

When you encounter a low-frequency person, the best first step is to try upping your frequency by saying positive things to them, showing support and offering kindness. These things can be enough to lift their frequency to yours. Sometimes, though, they're just not ready. This is when it might be better for you to create a little distance so that your frequency isn't lowered by theirs.

If you find yourself falling into low-frequency patterns with a particular person, you might be surprised at how much your energy levels and positivity rise when you've distanced yourself from them. Everybody is on their own journey through life, and it's important you make decisions that enable you to lead your own life.

How do you feel when you meet a high-frequency person after spending time with a low-frequency person?

....

....

....

....

....

What kind of people allow you to be your best, most positive self?

....

....

....

....

....

What kind of person do you want to be for the benefit of others?

....

....

....

....

....

What three things are you grateful for today?

....

....

....

What would you like to manifest today?

....

....

....

....

....

What message do you have for the universe?

....

....

....

....

....

A PERFECT DAY

This visualization exercise is a lot of fun and helps to underline what it is that you really want from life. To do it, find a place that's quiet where you won't be disturbed for 15–20 minutes. You can do it at any time of day, but it takes a bit of concentration, so practising in the morning when you have plenty of energy is a good idea.

In this exercise, you will close your eyes and play a mind movie of your perfect day. This isn't a once-in-a-lifetime day, such as marrying your dream partner (although of course that is a worthy visualization too!). Rather, it's a day where everything goes right for you and where you have everything you want.

Begin your perfect day by imagining waking up – where are you living? What is the weather like? What do you do first? Do you work in a dream job, create a dream project or volunteer in a life-changing role? Look at the people you interact with during your perfect day – what kinds of personalities do they have? How do they greet you? How do you greet them?

This exercise is fantastic for getting to the heart of what you want and who you want to spend time with. It might take a few attempts to overcome blocks that can limit our dreams, such as avoiding huge goals, but persevere.

What does your dream day look like?

....

....

....

....

....

....

....

....

....

....

....

How did this visualization make you feel?

....

....

....

....

....

What five things are you grateful for today?

....

....

....

....

....

What would you like to manifest today?

....

....

....

....

What message do you have for the universe?

....

....

....

....

MY LIFE
IS FILLED
WITH
ABUNDANCE

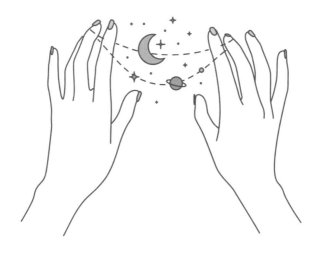

MANIFEST SOMETHING SMALL

When you're working towards big manifestations, a good way of staying focused and positive is to manifest small things alongside lofty things. This practice helps to raise your frequency on two levels: firstly, it shows the universe that you're determined, and secondly, it helps you appreciate the small things in life.

The small things you can manifest depend on you, but they should be simple and not things that you have blocks around. A great item to manifest is a book. Perhaps there's a title that someone recommended to you. If not, you can make it general and manifest a book you'll really enjoy. Take some time to visualize the cover (if you know it), how it'll feel to open the pages and turn them, the peace that reading brings and how animatedly you'll tell others about this book. Using multiple senses in your visualization helps to send a strong message to the universe.

Now, all you have to do is relinquish this desire to the universe and go about your daily life, trusting that this book will find its way to you. It might be in the window of your local library; you might spot it in your local second-hand shop; a friend might find it on their shelves and think you might like it. Whenever and however this small item finds you, take a moment to thank the universe for its work.

What small item(s) would you like to manifest?

....

....

....

....

What does this thing look, feel and sound like?

....

....

....

....

How will you feel when you receive what you've manifested?

....

....

....

....

Who will you tell about this manifestation success?

....

....

....

....

What three things are you grateful for today?

....

....

....

How do you feel about today's practice?

....

....

....

....

What message would you like to send back to the universe?

....

....

....

....

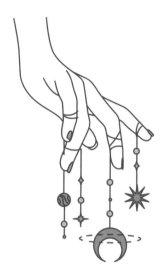

REMEMBER TO RELAX

We lead busy lives and experiencing some daily stress is natural. If we start worrying that we're manifesting incorrectly or it's not working properly, we're only adding extra stress into our lives that creates manifestation blocks. It's important to give yourself a break and aim to spend a little time each day relaxing. Self-care and relaxation raise your frequency, which in turn will open you up to opportunities and help the universe give you what you want.

Relaxation means different things to different people. Seeing close friends who make you laugh, going for walks in nature, snuggling on the sofa with a good book, watching feel-good movies and meditating are all common methods of relaxation. Engaging in these types of activities can help you step into the present moment, an act that lifts stress and floods you with energy.

Focusing on bringing a little relaxation into your life has other benefits too. It helps raise the frequencies of those who surround you, puts you in a perfect position to spot the opportunities the universe is presenting to you and makes space for you to be grateful for what you have in that very moment.

What activity do you find relaxing?

....

....

....

....

....

What does self-care mean to you?

....

....

....

....

....

How would a relaxed version of you behave in relationships and at work?

....

....

....

....

....

What five words describe that relaxed version of you?

....

....

....

....

....

What five things are you grateful for today?

....

....

....

....

....

What would you like to manifest today?

....

....

....

....

....

Your mind will answer most questions if you learn to relax and wait for the answer.

WILLIAM S. BURROUGHS

REDUCE STRESS

Stress is one of the biggest blocks when it comes to manifestation. While it is completely natural to feel stress, it's a problem when it's a constant companion. Chronic stress lowers our frequency, stops us from functioning at our best and prevents us from thinking clearly. When it comes to manifesting, it's vital that you address the stresses in your life and take steps to reduce them.

Try making a list of things that often raise your stress levels. These might include commuting to work, being worried about checking your bank balance or having to give presentations in your job. Go through each point and write down a couple of steps you could take to reduce that stress. Thinking proactively like this raises your frequency and lets the universe know that you're ready to tackle these issues.

Stressor: I feel stressed every time I must give a presentation or speak in front of a group of colleagues.

Steps I will take:

1. I will affirm to myself that "I am excited to give presentations and share my insightful knowledge".

2. I will practise my presentation ten times so I know it well.

3. Twice a day I will visualize giving my presentation and seeing my colleagues smiling and nodding along.

4. I will be thankful that my expertise is respected and sought after.

Five stress-reducing affirmations:

....

....

....

....

....

How will you feel when you start taking control of your stress levels?

....

....

....

....

What benefits will flood into your life when you're less stressed?

....

....

....

....

Who will benefit from a less stressed version of you?

....

....

....

....

What five things are you grateful for today?

....

....

....

....

....

What would you like to manifest today?

....

....

....

....

....

How do you feel after today's practice?

....

....

....

....

....

SCRIPTING LETTER

This popular technique is fantastic for focusing and sending a clear message to the universe. All you need to do this is a piece of paper and a pen.

This exercise involves writing a letter of thanks for all the things you have manifested. While these things are in your future, you will write the letter in the past or present tense, as though they have already come to be. Sit somewhere quiet and give yourself time to commit to this exercise – it will change your life!

Step 1: Address your letter to a higher being. This could be the universe, the Creator or whatever you feel is out there listening to you.

Step 2: Write down something you are thankful for as though you have already manifested it. Here's an example: "I now have a wonderful car that is safe, comfortable and reliable".

Step 3: Add a sentence explaining how this makes you feel, such as, "I am so joyful that I can now drive my children to their activities and help my neighbour with her shopping".

Step 4: Repeat for three or four things you are manifesting.

Step 5: Sign the letter off with more thanks.

Step 6: Read this letter every day, taking the time to pause on each point and really feel how wonderful it is to already have those things.

Here's a space to craft your scripting letter.

Dear ....

....

....

....

....

....

....

....

....

....

....

....

....

....

....

....

How will your scripted manifestations help those around you?

....

....

....

....

Where will you put your scripting letter so you can read it every day?

....

....

....

How do you feel about today's practice?

....

....

....

....

What message do you have for the universe?

....

....

....

....

Whether you think you can, or you think you can't – you're right.

HENRY FORD

AVOID LOW-VIBE BEHAVIOURS

While we can do plenty of things that raise our frequency and attract positivity into our lives, one of the best ways to help this happen is to avoid the things that drag our vibrations down in the first place. Just as talking to low-frequency people leaves us feeling deflated, *doing* low-frequency things also sets us back. It is often easy to work out what behaviour is low frequency – you don't feel good afterwards. Here are some examples of things that are commonly low frequency:

Criticizing: For a moment, you might scratch an itch when you criticize someone, but soon afterwards, you start feeling more negative than before.

Lying: While some lies help protect people – such as easing a child's worry – most are negative and lower your frequency. In contrast, when you tell the truth, you quickly feel a surge of relief, love and high frequency.

Eating unhealthily: Junk and ultra-processed foods unbalance the body's functioning, sending blood sugar skyrocketing and then crashing. Eating a balanced, healthy diet helps our bodies and shows the universe we are respecting ourselves.

Comparing: Whether scrolling through social media or looking up our friend's new house to see the sale price, comparing ourselves to others lowers our vibes. It's important to remember that we are all on our own journeys.

Five high-frequency behaviours you can work on:

....

....

....

....

....

How does it make you feel when you choose a high-vibe course of action?

....

....

....

....

Who will benefit when you raise your frequency?

....

....

....

....

How does the best version of you act?

....

....

....

....

What three things are you grateful for today?

....

....

....

What would you like to manifest this week?

....

....

....

....

How do you feel about today's practice?

....

....

....

....

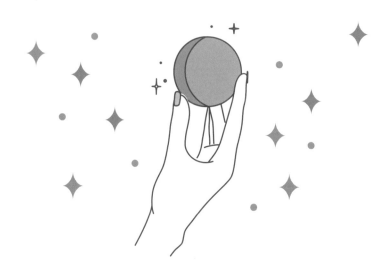

SUPPORT OTHERS

This is one of the most rewarding ways to raise your frequency and help manifest the things you want. It involves practising gratitude for the positive things that happen to other people and being generous with your support for them. This practice helps us to stop comparing ourselves to others and instead do whatever we can to help raise them up even further and achieve their goals.

One of the easiest ways to do this is to simply start congratulating others. This might be praising your friend for getting a promotion, your sister for running a race, a colleague for presenting their ideas or someone you follow online who has achieved something. Whenever you're tempted to ignore somebody's achievement because it elicits uncomfortable feelings such as envy or lack, consciously decide to take a deep breath and congratulate them. Soon, not only will congratulating people become a habit, but you will start naturally feeling joy for other people's achievements. This behaviour raises your frequency quickly and brings more joy into your life and into the lives of others.

Another way to support others is asking if you can do anything to help them. You might cook your partner their favourite meal when they have to work late, or give advice to somebody who's starting out in a field you know well.

Who can you congratulate this week?

....

....

....

....

Name five people you will support this week:

....

....

....

....

....

How does it make you feel to give help and advice to others?

....

....

....

....

Who will benefit when you make intentions to support others?

....

....

....

....

Who has supported you in the past?

....

....

....

....

How did it feel to be supported?

....

....

....

....

What five things are you grateful for today?

....

....

....

....

....

What would you like to manifest today?

....

....

....

....

I LOVE SHARING MY GIFTS WITH THE WORLD

BE SPECIFIC

Because we often struggle to believe that we will actually get what we want, particularly if it seems like a big deal, we aren't always very good at being specific. Perhaps you've been dreaming of a beautiful house in a great location. When it comes to manifesting these things, though, the universe can't support your desire of a dream house if it doesn't know exactly what that is. Remember, the first step to manifesting is to get some clarity.

Visualizing is not only a good way to send the universe a message about what you want but it's also a good way of working out what that thing is in the first place. When you have a vague idea of what it is you want, it's time to take one of those things and make some time and space to visualize the specifics. Want a house? Take a tour.

Close your eyes and begin in the street outside your new house. What kinds of buildings are on the street (if any)? Are there trees? Now, turn to look at your new home. What sort of house is it? What colour is the front door? As you make your way inside, what's the first thing you see? Is there carpet? What's your pet doing? Where does your best friend sit when they come round for dinner? The more specific you are, the clearer the message you send.

What would you like to manifest?

....
....
....
....

What are five words you associate with that thing?

....
....
....
....

Describe how it feels to have it in your near future.

....
....
....
....

How will you feel the day you get it?

....
....
....
....

What item could you carry with you that reminds you of that visualization?

....

....

What five things are you grateful for today?

....

....

....

....

....

How do you feel after today's practice?

....

....

....

....

....

A LETTER FROM FUTURE YOU

This is a fun scripting exercise similar to the thank-you letter, only this time it's from future you. All you need is a piece of paper (or a page in your journal) and a pen. It's better to handwrite this letter because it slows you down and allows you to really savour the feeling.

For this exercise, imagine that you are living sometime in the future. The scale or timeframe depends on what you're manifesting, but you could choose three, six or nine years, for example, as these are special numbers for the universe. Now, begin writing your letter to the person you are today, as though you're in the future and everything you are manifesting has come true. Explain to yourself just how amazing things are in the future, how successful you've been, what you're up to now and how much joy fills your days. Describe how the things you manifested have changed your life for the better.

This exercise is extremely powerful, and you'll be able to feel the high energy of it the moment you write the first sentence. Be as creative and detailed as you can, as this will help link your emotions to this future existence. When you're done, read the letter to yourself and put it somewhere safe so you can read it again every so often.

Describe three things that your future self has manifested successfully.

....

....

....

How does your future self feel about having these things?

....

....

....

....

....

What advice does your future self give to your present self?

....

....

....

....

....

What does your future self's day look like?

··

··

··

··

··

What three things are you grateful for?

··

··

··

How do you feel about today's practice?

··

··

··

··

··

EVERY DAY
THERE IS
MORE LOVE
IN MY LIFE

A LETTER TO YOUR PAST SELF

Writing a letter from future you is fun, inspiring and helps you manifest clearly. However, a letter to your past self is a brilliant way to spark gratitude and a feeling of abundance, and to raise your frequency as well. In this letter, you can choose a version of yourself far in the past, perhaps ten years or more, depending on your age now. Write to a past you who could only dream of the life you're leading now.

In this letter, describe the most wonderful things in your life today and let your past self know that all the struggles and challenges along the way helped you reach where you are right now. You might talk about how you met your best friend in an unlikely place or how you made the leap to change careers and learn new skills. These things can be smaller too. Perhaps you joined a local running club and take part in 5k events. Maybe you got a dog and feel endless love for it. Or it could be that you now wear red lipstick when back then you didn't have the confidence.

This letter is an exercise in developing and expressing gratitude. No matter where you are now, and no matter where you want to go, it helps show how far you've already come.

What are your five top achievements so far in life?

....

....

....

....

....

What five words describe your life right now?

....

....

....

....

....

What advice would you give to your past self?

....

....

....

....

....

What about yourself are you most proud of?

....

....

....

....

....

What five things are you grateful for today?

....

....

....

....

....

What would you like to manifest?

....

....

....

....

....

ABUNDANCE CHEQUES

A classic manifestation tool is the cheque. These days, it's less and less likely that you have a real chequebook at all – perhaps you've never had one! But cheques are still a great tool in manifestation. Jim Carrey is a famous example of someone who has used this technique: before he was famous, he wrote himself a cheque for US$10 million for "acting services rendered". Within five years, he was earning that much. Cheques are ideal for manifesting money because they're a traditional financial tool, but you can write anything you want on your abundance cheque.

An easy way to get a cheque is to do an internet search for "blank abundance cheque". You'll soon find images to download and print. Alternatively, you could get creative and make your own version. Now, all you need to do is write yourself that cheque. Simply write in the amount of money you want, put a date a little way into the future and then sign it.

Put the cheque in a place where you'll see it often and believe that the money is already working its way towards you.

What does manifesting money mean to you?

....

....

....

....

....

How do you feel when you look at your abundance cheque?

....

....

....

....

....

What five words would you use to describe the day you receive the amount you wrote on the cheque?

....

....

....

....

....

Who will you tell about your manifestation cheque success?

....

....

....

....

Who will benefit from your abundance cheque?

....

....

....

....

What five things are you grateful for today?

....

....

....

....

What message would you like to give the universe?

....

....

....

....

As far as I can tell, it's just about letting the universe know what you want and then working towards it while letting go of how it comes to pass.

JIM CARREY

SEEK HELP

Negative talk can derail manifestation, so it's important that you take note of it. Because we're people of habit, enlisting someone to help us spot slip-ups is a great idea. The best person for this will be a supportive person you talk to a lot. A friend, a partner or a family member is usually the best bet.

Explain that you want to reduce negativity by changing the way you talk about things. Every time they hear you say something negative, they'll bring it to your attention. There's no judgement here, and you won't be "failing" by saying something negative. Instead, this helpful nudge will allow you to *hear* yourself. Here are some examples of things your friend might catch you saying:

- "I have to go to my brother's dinner party, but his friends are so annoying."

- "There's no point in applying for that job because I don't meet all the criteria."

- "The traffic will be awful and I'll never find a parking space."

When we get into the habit of being negative, we interpret everything as negative. By having someone kindly point out when we've slipped into negative talk, we can acknowledge it and rephrase it into a positive: "Applying for the job is great practice and gets my name in front of their HR. Plus, I know I can learn anything they need me to."

Five affirmations that will help you reduce negativity:

....

....

....

....

....

People you could ask for help and the ways in which they could support you:

....

....

....

....

....

Who will benefit from your new positivity?

....

....

....

....

....

How will you feel when you reframe things positively?

....

....

....

....

....

What are you excited to manifest?

....

....

....

....

....

What three things are you grateful for today?

....

....

....

....

....

PRACTISE MEDITATION

Because the law of attraction works when you are in a positive frame of mind, it's important that you take the time to calm your thoughts and allow positivity in. One of the best ways to do this is through meditation. An ancient practice, meditation involves bringing your mind into the present moment where thoughts can come and go without you holding on to them and getting distracted.

Meditation takes practice, and MRI-based studies have shown that it changes the functioning of the brain. That's right, you're literally changing your brain by meditating! Meditation may feel close to impossible at first, so it's best to start with a simple breathing meditation.

- Sit comfortably in a place you won't be disturbed.

- Close your eyes and focus on your breathing.

- Begin counting your breaths: inhale one, exhale two, inhale three, exhale four, etc.

- When you reach ten, begin again from one.

- As thoughts come into your head, acknowledge them and let them go, returning your attention to counting breaths.

- Some days will bring more distracting thoughts than others, but over time you'll find it easier to let your thoughts go.

- After finishing your meditation, perhaps ten minutes or so, you can continue with another manifestation exercise, knowing that your mind is calm.

What five words do you associate with meditation practice?

....

....

....

....

....

How might you benefit from having a calmer mind?

....

....

....

....

What time of day do you intend on meditating?

....

....

Where will you meditate?

....

....

....

How does meditating make you feel afterwards?

....

....

....

....

What five things are you grateful for today?

....

....

....

....

What would you like to manifest today with a calmer mind?

....

....

....

....

WITH EVERY
BREATH I TAKE,
I AM LETTING
PEACE INTO
MY BODY

SLEEP ON IT

This scripting technique takes the advice your mother probably gave you quite literally. On a piece of paper, you'll write down something that you want to manifest. Go into as much detail as you like and describe how you feel knowing that it's coming to you. When you're done, place the paper under your pillow when you go to bed and, literally, sleep on it!

In the morning, place the paper somewhere safe, such as a bedside table, and take it back out again at night. Read it through and then place it back under your pillow so it's fresh in your mind as you go to sleep. Repeat this for a month and trust that the universe will be busy turning your desire into a reality.

What are you excited to script?

....

....

....

....

How will you feel when you wake up knowing the universe has your back?

....

....

....

....

What emotions will you feel when you receive what you've asked for?

....

....

....

....

Where will you place your script during the day to keep it safe and cared for?

....

....

....

How do you feel about today's practice?

....

....

....

....

What five things are you grateful for today?

....

....

....

....

....

What do you want the universe to know?

....

....

....

....

SEEING AND USING ANGEL NUMBERS

Have you ever seen the same time on your clock every day? Perhaps 11:11 or 22:22? The concept of "angel numbers" – or "manifestation numbers" – comes up time and again in manifestation. It refers to patterns of numbers that keep appearing in your life. For many, angel numbers are a marker that show you're on the right path, or they serve as reminders to have faith. The numbers are usually trios of identical numbers like 111 or 333. If you often see 666, don't worry, it's actually a positive angel number too!

When you see an angel number, you probably pause immediately. After all, repeated numbers are quite notable even if you've never heard of angel numbers before, and you've probably pointed out to someone that the time is 11:11 or 22:22 in the past. Because these numbers already give you pause, it's a perfect time to consciously reconnect with the universe. You can do this by making an affirmation, thanking the universe or visualizing what you're manifesting. When you catch it on the fly while doing something else, such as driving, a quick "thank you for having my back" to the universe is ideal.

What numbers do you notice coming up again and again in your life?

....
....
....
....

Which number or numbers have the strongest pull for you?

....
....
....
....

What time of day do you feel most energized and positive?

....
....
....

How do you feel when you see numbers that are special to you?

....
....
....
....

What are you excited to manifest today?

....

....

....

....

What will you do next time you see an angel number?

....

....

....

....

What five things are you grateful for today?

....

....

....

....

....

How do you feel about today's practice?

....

....

....

....

*If you can
see it in
your mind,
you will hold it
in your hand.*

BOB PROCTOR

WHEN THE GOING GETS TOUGH

It's no surprise that visualizing, scripting and feeling powerful positive emotions is easier when we're in a good mood. But what happens when your mind darkens and sadness takes the driving seat? This is a completely normal thing to happen to us all from time to time. Luckily, gratitude and affirmations offer a source of solace.

Often when we're sad, we have repeating negative thoughts. Maybe something went wrong at work and you've spent the afternoon feeling like you don't belong in your role, or perhaps you spotted your partner laughing with someone and it fired up fears and insecurities. Sometimes our brains leap to worst-case scenarios, thinking they're protecting us. The best thing to do in these situations is to halt those thoughts by filling your mind with new ones. This is where affirmations come in.

Having a few emergency affirmations on your phone is a great idea. When you catch yourself falling into a negative thought pattern, you can whip out your phone and repeat your affirmations. If you have a therapist, working on some appropriate affirmations with them will fortify you as well. Here are some examples:

- "I know the universe has my back and that all is well."

- "I am safe and loved."

- "I know this feeling will pass and be replaced with light and positivity."

Five positive affirmations that can lift you out of a funk:

....

....

....

....

....

Which high-frequency friend could you call to help lift your energy?

....

....

....

....

....

What high-frequency activities can you do when you need to
up your vibe?

....

....

....

....

....

How does the most positive version of you react to challenging times?

....

....

....

....

....

What would you like to manifest today?

....

....

....

....

....

What three things are you grateful for today?

....

....

....

....

....

CHANGE IS GOOD

As the saying goes, "If you keep doing the same thing, then you'll keep getting the same result". Using manifestation techniques regularly will help you change your mindset and open up opportunities for you, but to position yourself to take advantage of them, practising getting out of your comfort zone is important.

Most of us have quite routine-based lives. We might work five days a week, have a sport club on a Wednesday, takeaway on a Friday and laundry day every Sunday. There's nothing wrong with routine as it frees our minds up for other things. But when long periods of time go by without doing anything new, it's harder for the universe to put positive change in our path.

With this in mind, try doing something new once a week. It might be eating a different food, going to a new workout class or talking to a new person at work. You never know where these things might take you.

What five new things would you like to do?

....

....

....

....

....

What's the first step to doing each of those five things?

....

....

....

....

Which one are you most excited to try and why?

....

....

....

....

How do you feel when you've challenged yourself with something new?

....

....

....

....

....

What would you like to manifest today?

....

....

....

....

What five things are you grateful for today?

....

....

....

....

....

I TAKE OWNERSHIP OF MY LIFE AND PURSUE MY DREAMS EVERY DAY

TRACK YOUR WINS

If you're manifesting something larger than a nice cup of coffee, chances are it'll happen in stages. This is one of the reasons why those new to manifesting can feel frustrated when nothing appears to be happening – they're looking for the end result and not evidence of progress. Once you start looking for progress, though, you'll start seeing it everywhere. Keeping track of the manifestation wins will soon show you how the universe is plotting your biggest manifestations. So, how do you spot the steps of success? Here's an example of what manifestation progress might look like.

Manifestation: I want to be a bestselling author.

Potential steps the universe takes:
- Your child joins an activity club that means you have to wait in a café for an hour every week.

- Your local library starts running author talks.

- You find a few recent bestsellers in a second-hand shop.

At first, it might not seem like any of these are helping you become a bestselling author, but actually, all of them are. You can dedicate that café hour to writing. By attending author talks, you can learn about the writer's process and ask them questions. Reading bestsellers teaches you what fiction sells and exposes you to plot lines and characterization.

Whenever you spot a manifestation win, write it down and track the progress. You'll be amazed.

What is your biggest accomplishment to date, and what are some of the steps that led you to it?

··

··

··

··

What major thing would you like to manifest?

··

··

··

··

What are a few of the steps you could take that could help you along the way?

··

··

··

What has already happened to open up the first door for you?

....

....

....

....

How will you feel when you start seeing progress towards your manifestation goal?

....

....

....

....

What three things are you grateful for today?

....

....

....

How do you feel about today's practice?

....

....

....

55 x 5 TECHNIQUE

This is a popular manifestation scripting technique that is fast-acting. It involves focusing on one particular manifestation and writing it down 55 times every day for five days. This intensity sends a very clear message to the universe as well as to your own mind, so you're in the best position possible to spot opportunities related to what you desire.

When you start this exercise, it's wise to write a concise manifestation. After all, you'll be writing it 55 times every day! So, keep it concise but also specific. When it's specific, it's easier to visualize and therefore easier for the universe to understand. As you're aiming to make progress in a short period of time, keep it realistic for this type of timeframe too.

The key to this technique is to write your manifestation down in the present tense: for example, "I landed my dream role as a people manager", or "I landed a literary agent for my novel". This updates your brain to accept that this is not only possible but is happening.

Each day, take a piece of lined paper and make a mark where the 55th line will be. You might want to draw a line down the centre to make two columns and even go onto the back! This means you won't need to count while you're writing. Handwrite your manifestation 55 times and put it away. Repeat for five days.

What are you excited to manifest in this exercise?

....

....

....

....

Where will you write your 55 × 5 exercise?

....

....

....

....

How will you feel when you see progress towards this goal?

....

....

....

....

Who else will benefit from your manifestation?

....

....

....

....

Three steps you can take to help the universe make this manifestation come true:

....

....

....

What five things are you grateful for today?

....

....

....

....

....

Describe your primary emotion right now.

....

....

....

....

....

To bring anything into your life, imagine that it's already there.

RICHARD BACH

GOAL PICTURES

This is a visualization technique popularized by Jack Canfield, the author of *Chicken Soup for the Soul*. It involves creating a picture of you having achieved your goal and is a type of tangible visualization. You might need to get a little creative depending on what your goal is. If you want to find and buy your dream home, go out and track down a house that matches what you're looking for. Get your partner or a supportive friend to take a picture of you in front of the house, holding up a set of house keys as though you just bought it. If you want to manifest confidence, try taking a selfie of you standing in Superman pose.

When you have a photograph of yourself that represents what you want to manifest, print it out and put it somewhere you see every day. A big manifestation block is that while we know what we want, we don't actually *believe* that it's possible for *us*. This technique works wonders because it directly contradicts your negative self-belief by showing you that the person who owns that house and who exudes confidence is actually you! A popular saying in the manifestation community is "Thoughts become things". So, when you start thinking of yourself as a homeowner or a confident person, it won't be long until reality follows.

What is your primary manifestation goal for this exercise?

··

··

··

··

How will you go about creating or taking an image of yourself having successfully manifested that thing?

··

··

··

··

Who will benefit from this manifestation coming true?

··

··

··

··

How will you feel when you see that image?

··

··

··

··

Where will you put your image so you can see it often?

....

....

....

....

....

What three things are you grateful for today?

....

....

....

How do you feel knowing that your dreams will come true?

....

....

....

....

....

THE TIME IS NOW

There is absolutely a right time to manifest, and that time is now. But that's not to say you should just script or visualize what you're manifesting now; it's vital that you take the first step right now too. By telling the universe what you want and then taking immediate action, you're showing that you're serious, committed and ready to receive it. But how exactly do you take action when you're not sure how you can get what you want in the first place?

If you're manifesting a new partner, the first step might be to expand your social circle so you can meet new people. You could look for interesting courses to sign up to, accept invitations you might normally skip or join a dating site. Simply telling your friends that you're ready to start a new relationship can be a great first step too, as they can help you spot opportunities to meet new people, or they might realize they know a perfect match. If you're not sure what first step to take, sometimes a good old-fashioned Google search will provide the answers: "how to make new friends as an adult", or "unique first date ideas". While you might not find the perfect answer for you, you'll almost certainly get some inspiration.

By taking the next step, you're showing yourself that you are willing to put in the work to make your desires a reality.

What are three things you want to manifest?

....

....

....

What are the first steps you can take for each of those things?

....

....

....

Who could help you take these first steps?

....

....

....

....

What time today will you start working on these steps?

....

....

....

How will it feel to make progress towards your manifestation goals?

....

....

....

....

What five things are you grateful for today?

....

....

....

....

....

Draw a quick sketch of your expression when you take your first steps.

ALL I NEED
IS WITHIN
ME RIGHT
NOW

SHOW YOUR WEALTH YOU CARE

If you're manifesting wealth and money, it's useful to work out if you're sending it the right signals. Lots of us have complex relationships with money, due to conflicting messages we received when we were young. We might also be giving out conflicting messages with our behaviour towards money.

Picture this: you get paid and the next day you decide to get lunch out. The delicious café down the road feels a little far, so you pop round the corner and buy a mediocre, overpriced sandwich. Later, you take some money out of the ATM and put it in your pocket instead of your wallet. When you get home, you realize you didn't close your pocket and the money must have fallen out. In both instances, you haven't taken very good care of the money. What message does that send out? Not a positive one.

When manifesting money, it's important to treat the money you have with care, love and respect. That doesn't mean hoarding it and not spending any; money isn't for burying any more than it is for wasting. It means making intentional, well-thought-out purchases that raise your frequency and show money that you care about where it goes. This practice also requires knowing where your money is and how much you have. Spreadsheets and tracker apps are great for this.

Five positive wealth affirmations:

....

....

....

....

....

How will being wealthy make you feel?

....

....

....

....

Who else will benefit from your new wealth?

....

....

....

....

Three things you can do when you have the money you manifest:

....

....

....

How will you show your current money that you love and care for it?

....

....

....

....

Whose advice might you seek in learning more about managing money?

....

....

....

....

What five things are you grateful for today?

....

....

....

....

How has today's practice made you feel?

....

....

....

....

TRUST YOUR GUT

When you've been manifesting and are waiting for things to begin changing, you may be looking out for the end result. We already covered spotting the small steps that indicate progress, but there's something else you need to look out for: gut instinct. There are a lot of forces at work in the universe that you can't see. However, when you tune in to your gut – your second brain – you're much more likely to pick up on the ways the universe is trying to help you.

Have you ever made a snap decision based on a feeling? Maybe it was to say yes to an event you would never normally go to, or perhaps you needed directions and your gut told you which stranger to ask. If you think back, you may well find that it was that gut instinct that led you to an opportunity: you met a mentor at that event, or that stranger turned into your future partner, best friend or new colleague.

Gut feelings aren't random and should never be ignored. They won't always lead to something life-changing, but when your gut tries to get your attention, there's usually a reason. If you always make a point to listen to it, then you can decide if it's worth acting on or if it just needs a little love that day.

List two times that you have acted on gut instinct and it turned out to be right:

....

....

....

....

....

How do you feel about trusting your gut?

....

....

....

....

....

What do your instincts tend to be most attuned to?

....

....

....

....

....

What are you excited to start manifesting today?

....

....

....

Which friends or family members can you ask about their gut-instinct experiences?

....

....

....

....

What five things are you grateful for today?

....

....

....

....

What does your life look like when you're in tune with your instincts?

....

....

....

MY INTUITION GROWS STRONGER EVERY DAY

THE UNIVERSE KNOWS PEOPLE

With all this talk of signs, angel numbers and gut instincts, it's understandable to worry about missing indicators. If you don't follow your instinct and miss the relevance of a sign, does that mean your manifestation won't come true? No. It's okay. You can relax. The universe understands us better than we understand ourselves; it knows we can be slow on the uptake even if we *asked* for the thing it's dangling in front of us. Sometimes we just can't see the wood for the trees.

When you're worried about missing opportunities or wondering why your manifestations are taking so long, it's probably time to simply trust that the universe will find a way. If you miss an open door to opportunity, the universe knows that next time it'll have to open it wider and maybe play your favourite song at the same time.

When you stop worrying and start trusting the process, you create the space you need in your awareness to see the opportunities you're afraid of missing. When the time is right, you'll see what you need to see, and you'll feel compelled to take the action you need to take. Have faith.

What does the version of you who completely trusts the universe think when manifestation takes a while?

....

....

....

....

Three affirmations for patience and faith:

....

....

....

Describe how it feels to know that the universe will catch you when you slip.

....

....

....

....

What does your life need more of?

....

....

....

....

What five things are you grateful for today?

....

....

....

....

....

What can you focus on today that will build your faith in the universe?

....

....

....

....

....

How do you feel about today's practice?

....

....

....

....

....

GET INTO A GRATITUDE LOOP

When you recognize that your manifestations are beginning to work – perhaps you've spotted signs of progress or a new opportunity has arisen – remember to thank the universe and be grateful. If you feel the confidence to sign up to a dating app or to visit a mortgage broker, thank the universe. Nothing is too small to be thankful for. When you practise gratitude on this level, you develop a greater awareness about what's going on in your life and keep your frequency high. This in turn keeps the law of attraction drawing more high-frequency things into your life, creating a gratitude loop.

There are few things more powerful than being in a gratitude loop, and it feels immensely positive. You start feeling thankful for everything and cherishing the abundance in your life. You can manifest bigger things with this power, but you can also feel a sweeping contentedness knowing that whenever you need something, the universe has your back.

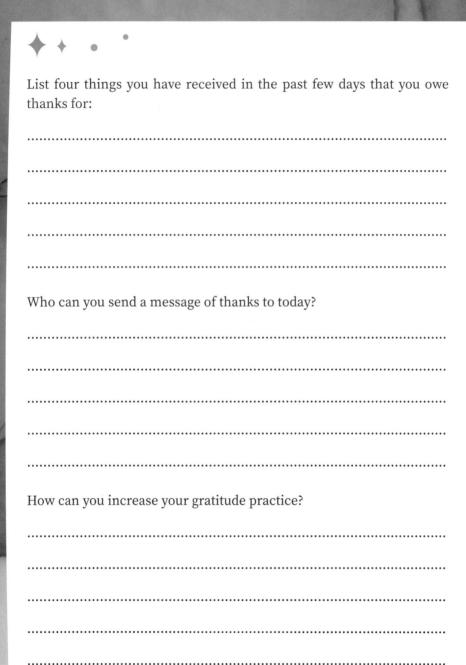

List four things you have received in the past few days that you owe thanks for:

....

....

....

....

Who can you send a message of thanks to today?

....

....

....

....

How can you increase your gratitude practice?

....

....

....

....

....

What five things are you particularly grateful for today?

....

....

....

....

....

How does it make you feel when somebody takes the time to thank you?

....

....

....

....

....

What are you excited to manifest in your life today?

....

....

....

....

....

Gratitude opens the door, the power, the wisdom, the creativity of the universe. You open the door through gratitude.

DEEPAK CHOPRA

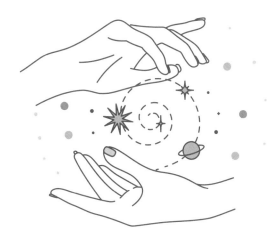

FIND A BUDDY

Manifestation is a personal journey because it's all about the things you want most in your life. That's not to say you should only do it alone though. Having a friend who you can talk to about your manifestation practices and share tips with can help you manifest more effectively! Sharing your manifestation journey can build a stronger friendship as you're both going through something challenging and exciting together, even when you're manifesting totally different things. Close relationships based in positivity and mutual support are fantastic for raising your frequency.

Knowing who to talk to about manifestation might be difficult, particularly if your friends are a little sceptical about esoteric things. A good way to broach it might be to talk about visualization first. This is a world-renowned psychological technique used by Olympic athletes and is frequently talked about. It's easy for most people to see the benefits of creative visualization, so this is a great place to start a mutual manifestation journey.

Many of your friends will probably have already heard about manifestation and might have even read books that are based on it. Friends tend to have a lot of things in common and think about things in similar ways, so you might well find your friends are queueing up to talk manifestation tips and tricks!

Who could you talk to about joining you on a manifestation journey?

....

....

....

What would it mean to you to share your experiences?

....

....

....

....

How do you feel when a friend confides in you?

....

....

....

How does it feel to confide in others?

....

....

....

....

What three things are you grateful for today?

....

....

....

What would you like to manifest this week?

....

....

....

....

How will you feel when you have what you desire?

....

....

....

....

DON'T WORRY ABOUT THE TIMING

We live in an instant-gratification society where we can contact each other, buy things and even start businesses with the click of a button. But there are many things that still need time and patience. You might already know this. Perhaps you missed an opportunity when you were younger that you've recently taken, only to realize that you wouldn't have made the most of it had you taken it the first time around. It's easy to be impatient, but sometimes we're just not ready yet.

The universe works on a different timescale to us; it is, after all, infinite. You might think that you want or need your desire to manifest within a certain deadline, but if it doesn't happen despite no obstacles being in the way, chances are the universe just knows the time isn't right. If you're waiting for your great love, maybe you need to learn to give yourself love first. If you're waiting for the perfect role, perhaps someone else needs to move on to a different company beforehand. If you're waiting for a shiny new car, it might be that yours needs to break down to allow the mechanic to recommend the perfect replacement. You just never know.

The "perfect" timing for us is just something we invent with the limited knowledge and expectations we have. It's time to trust in the process.

Five affirmations you can say when you feel impatient:

....

....

....

....

....

Describe how you'll feel when your manifestations come true.

....

....

....

....

....

Write down a time when something came to you later than you expected, but it turned out to be the best timing.

....

....

....

....

....

What would you say to a friend who was worried their manifestations weren't happening fast enough?

....

....

....

....

....

What three things are you grateful for today?

....

....

....

What message would you like to send the universe right now?

....

....

....

....

....

SEEK MANIFESTATION STORIES

While you're waiting for your manifestations to be realized, seek out the manifestation success stories of others. This is a fantastic way of seeing just how diverse everybody's journeys are and the weird and wonderful ways the universe works its power. While manifesting is personal to each individual, there are plenty of commonalities. Most people manifest in the same broad categories: wealth, love, work, health, success. As a result, it's easy to find stories that are relevant and inspiring for you.

There are plenty of books out there containing the manifestation stories of others, as well as YouTube videos detailing extraordinary manifestation successes. What's so wonderful about these stories is that the community are supportive, positive and generous with their time and experiences. Surrounding yourself with stories of positivity, particularly when it comes from unexpected avenues, is a brilliant and enjoyable way to raise your frequency and attract more abundance into your life.

When you have your own manifestation stories, remember to share them widely!

Three things you've manifested in your life, even if you didn't realize it at the time:

....

....

....

What steps will you take to seek out other people's manifestation success stories?

....

....

....

....

....

How could you arrange your days so positivity surrounds you?

....

....

....

....

....

What five things are you grateful for today?

....

....

....

....

....

What would you like to manifest today?

....

....

....

....

....

What five words describe how you feel about your future?

....

....

....

....

....

FINAL WORD

Manifesting is a universal tool you can use to prepare yourself to live the life you dream about. It helps you find clarity to understand what you want in the first place and primes your mind to start seeing opportunities everywhere you look. While encouraging you to surround yourself with high-frequency people who can support your journey, it guides you towards the actions that make your desires a reality.

Throughout this journal, you have learned so much about manifestation and the law of attraction, and hopefully you've seen plenty of progress already. With the tips and prompts you've read you can continue your manifestation journey knowing exactly what you need to do to build the life you want no matter what happens. With trust, patience and an open mind, you are in the right place to see all the opportunities the universe presents to you and have the confidence to take them.

Good luck on your manifestation journey!

Have you enjoyed this book?
If so, find us on Facebook at **Summersdale Publishers**,
on Twitter at **@Summersdale** and on Instagram at
@summersdalebooks and get in touch.
We'd love to hear from you!

www.summersdale.com

IMAGE CREDITS